EFFECTIVE
SURVIVAL STRATEGIES™

# *Defeating*
# ADDICTION AND
# ALCOHOLISM

SUSAN HENNEBERG

ROSEN
PUBLISHING®

New York

Published in 2016 by The Rosen Publishing Group, Inc.
29 East 21st Street, New York, NY 10010

Copyright © 2016 by The Rosen Publishing Group, Inc.

First Edition

**Library of Congress Cataloging-in-Publication Data**

Henneberg, Susan.
 Defeating addiction and alcoholism / Susan Henneberg. — First edition.
     pages cm. — (Effective survival strategies)
 Includes bibliographical references and index.
 ISBN 978-1-4994-6179-4 (library bound)
 1. Substance abuse—Juvenile literature. 2. Substance abuse—Treatment—Juvenile literature.
 3. Alcoholism—Juvenile literature. 4. Alcoholism—Treatment—Juvenile literature. I. Title.
 RC564.3.H46 2016
 616.86—dc23
                        2015022419

For many of the images in this book, the people photographed are models. The depictions do not imply actual situations or events.

*Manufactured in China*

# Contents

# Introduction

Zac Efron quietly checked himself into a substance abuse rehab facility in 2013. Demi Lovato was more public about her reason for entering treatment. "I couldn't go 30 minutes to an hour without cocaine," the singer told *Access Hollywood* in 2013. She spent several months in rehab when she was nineteen. By the time Lindsay Lohan was twenty-seven, she had cycled in and out of treatment six times. *Glee* fans mourned the death of Cory Monteith of a heroin overdose in 2013. Celebrity addiction stories are everywhere. Rehab has become trendy, even glamorous.

Celebrities are the public face of substance abuse and addiction. However, many teens are just as familiar with the private world of drug dependence and alcoholism. They have an alcoholic parent. They know a friend who binge drinks every weekend. They hear stories about acquaintances who regularly take prescription pain pills. A coworker snorts cocaine in the restroom during breaks.

The statistics are sobering. According to the National Survey on Drug Use and Health (NSDUH), almost 3 percent of youth between twelve and seventeen in 2013 were dependent on or abused alcohol. Young adults aged eighteen to twenty-five added another 13 percent. Nearly 11 percent of youth and young adults between twelve and twenty-five were dependent on or

Singer Demi Lovato has been open about her battles with drug and alcohol abuse. Since treatment at age nineteen, Lovato has spoken out against the glamorizing of drug use in popular music.

abused illicit drugs. Six million children live with a parent who has a drug addiction.

Many teens experiment with underage drinking and illicit drugs. They grow into responsible adulthood. What pushes some teens into addiction? The reasons are complex. Most addiction experts agree that biology has a role to play. A tendency toward addiction can be part of a person's genetic inheritance. Some teens have poor impulse control or mental health issues. Environment is a major factor. Some teens suffer from personal or family trauma. They are exposed to overwhelming stress and lack support.

While celebrities check in and out of expensive rehab facilities, treatment is not as available for teens. The NSDUH survey revealed that only 10 percent of twelve- to seventeen-year-olds needing substance abuse treatment receive any services. Individual and group counseling can be effective for many teens. Inpatient and outpatient services are accessible for those families that can afford them. For more severe cases, teens may need to find residential programs. Most rehab facilities have small programs for youth. There are few solely teen-oriented residential options.

As teens rely on their phones and tablets for information and connection, substance abuse treatment has increasingly become available in digital forms. Teens can find smartphone apps that reinforce their commitment to sobriety. They can access web-based courses that teach them refusal skills and coping strategies. Online groups can provide added support for teens who benefit from social interaction.

Recognizing that the fifty-year war on drugs has been a failure, the United States is changing its approach to the problem of substance abuse and addiction. Researchers are honing in on the brain biology of addiction. Access to health care has improved. Doctors and therapists are using technology tools to provide more and better options to help teens struggling with sobriety. Teens and young adults can not only survive addiction but can thrive in their growth toward a productive and sober adulthood.

# CHAPTER 1

# AM I ADDICTED?

**T**eens today live in a drug-filled world. Giant billboards and glossy magazine ads connect alcohol with a glamorous lifestyle. On TV shows, characters take pills to cure not only illness and disease but also boredom and unhappiness. According to some celebrities, more is better when it comes to drugs. Teens absorb these messages at the time in which they are most prone to take risks.

During adolescence, the decision-making part of the brain is still developing. Teens often make choices based on emotion or peer pressure. They want to look cool and fit in. They want to avoid their problems and escape stress. They want to have fun. The Substance Abuse and Mental Health Services Administration (SAMHSA) surveys teens every year. In 2013 it showed that 27 percent of youth aged twelve to seventeen reported using illicit drugs in the past year. Of high school seniors, 37 percent admitted to drinking alcohol and 9.5 percent used narcotics.

These statistics are alarming. Substance use puts teens at risk for traffic accidents, risky sexual behavior, and violence. Poor health habits formed during adolescence often last forever.

Even more frightening, substance use can lead to abuse and addiction.

## What Does It Mean to Be an Addict?

Addiction experts define the word using medical terms. They say addiction is primary. That means it is not caused by any other disease. It is chronic. That means it can last a lifetime. An addiction can be controlled but not cured. It is a disease of the brain. Drugs change the brain's structure and how it works. These substances take over the brain's reward system so that nothing is as important as feeding the craving for the drugs.

According to the National Institute on Drug Abuse (NIDA), "These brain changes can be long lasting and can lead to many harmful, often self-destructive, behaviors." Substance abusers

Drug abusers soon find that they need more and more of the substance to achieve the same high. As they become desperate to score more, they fall into a downward spiral. Some teens even turn to selling drugs in order to afford their addiction.

develop tolerance. They need to take more and more to feel the same high. They cannot cut down or control their use of the substance. They spend a lot of time finding, using, and recovering from the effects of the abuse. Drug use causes school, social, and personal problems. Abusers suffer from withdrawal symptoms when they stop using the drug.

The American Psychiatric Association has stopped using the word "addiction." Its diagnostic manual replaces it with the term "substance use disorder" (SUD). Whatever this condition is called, compulsive drug seeking costs Americans more than $700 billion a year in increased health care costs, lost productivity, and crime. Addiction costs more than cancer, diabetes, and asthma combined.

## What Causes Addiction?

Substance use disorder is a complex disease. There is no simple answer to who becomes addicted. Some factors are biological. Other factors are environmental. No one knows how these factors mix.

Researchers have shown that alcoholism and drug addiction run in families. Children can inherit a tendency to addiction or substance use disorder. Some families have several addictions. Family members may eat, gamble, or hoard to excess. Researchers are studying the DNA of people who become substance dependent. They are looking at the role of particular genes. For instance, an area on chromosome 11 is associated with seeking new experiences. It lies near a region that has been linked to addiction. Carrying the genes for substance abuse does not mean that a person will become an abuser, however.

Having a certain personality may make some people lean toward substance abuse. These traits don't cause someone to become dependent, but they are found in many addicts. Their brains show differences in the areas involved in self-control. These people may not easily receive the message to stop drinking or doing drugs.  One common behavior trait among substance abusers is compulsivity. Sometimes this looks like perfectionism. Often it means that addicts cannot easily stop doing something that may be destructive. Another trait is impulsivity. Potential substance abusers take risks. They act without thinking and seek excitement. Feeling anxious and being antisocial are other traits.

Many substance abusers fit a certain personality type. They crave excitement, love to take risks, and act impulsively. However, there are also plenty of impulsive people who do not become addicts. Having this personality type does not mean you will become an addict.

None of these personality traits will lead a person to drinking or drug use unless there are outside factors. One big influence is home and family. Teens may not be well-supervised. Children are at greater risk for addiction if their parents suffer from dependence or mental illness, or engage in crime. Teens can get drugs if family members have prescription medicines in the house. A chaotic or violent household may cause stress for the children, leading to early drug use.

Other factors include social and peer influences and school performance. Having friends who abuse drugs may have a big impact on teen drug use. Poor grades in school may be a result of drug use. Bad grades may lead to low self-esteem and poor

Strong bonds between children and parents help teens become disciplined and self-confident. They are able to resist peer pressure to abuse drugs and alcohol.

choices. These issues all impact teens' social networks. Teens who have close bonds with successful adults can resist peer pressure.

Experts suspect that genes, personality, and environment led to the death of Bobbi Kristina Brown in 2015. The daughter of singers Whitney Houston and Bobby Brown, Bobbi Kristina was twenty-one when she was found unresponsive in her bathtub. Her mother had died in 2012 of a mix of a drug overdose and heart disease. News reports describe Bobbi Kristina's childhood as one filled with her parents' drug problems and domestic violence.

# THE IMPACT OF CELEBRITY

In our society, actors, musicians, athletes, and reality show stars control public opinion. They decide what is cool and popular. Teens especially want to copy their idols. When these public figures get out of control with drugs and alcohol, their behavior is covered widely by the media. It is easy for teens to get confused when these celebrities seem to be rewarded with a stay in a posh rehab facility. Young fans don't see that music and movie producers behind the scenes are passing up on passed-out celebs. Successful professionals look for more stable superstars who can get to work on time and who provide less drama. Think about who your heroes are and why. It's just possible that your parents and teachers are better role models than that movie star or rapper you like.

# The Addicted Brain

Medical researchers have learned a lot about the brain's role in addiction. Substance abuse causes lasting changes in the brain that are hard to reverse. One change involves neurotransmitters. These are tiny chemicals in the brain that communicate with different neurons. Another change is in the pleasure center in the brain, called the nucleus accumbens. People live to fulfill needs and desires, such as for food and love. When someone satisfies a need, the neurotransmitter dopamine is released in the nucleus accumbens and produces pleasure.

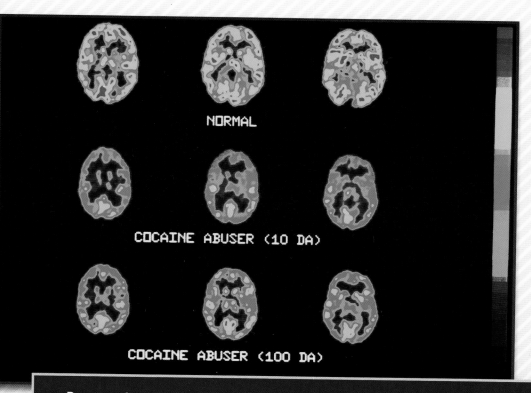

Drugs such as cocaine have a powerful effect on the brain. They can affect the areas of the brain that are responsible for judgment, learning, and memory, as shown by these brain scans.

This pleasurable reward usually comes with time and effort. Addictive drugs provide a shortcut. They flood the pleasure center with dopamine. The brain is soon unable to produce dopamine naturally. It needs the drugs. For instance, THC, the mind-altering chemical in marijuana, triggers brain cells to release dopamine. THC has a strong impact in the part of the brain called the hippocampus. This area is important in learning. Disrupting its normal functioning can lead to problems with studying and learning new things.

The brain creates associations between drug experiences and where and when they occurred. Whenever substance abusers find reminders of the experiences, the memories trigger a craving for the drugs. Even after a substance abuser spends years of living sober, these cravings can cause a relapse.

Teens are more prone to addiction because of their brain development. The part of the brain that makes good decisions is the prefrontal cortex. This area develops slower than the areas that control pleasure and risk. It's as if the "go" areas of the brain mature earlier than the "stop." A maturing adolescent learns to put the brakes on too much risk.

# CHAPTER 2

# WHEN DRUG USE ESCALATES

Hip hop and soul singer Mary J. Blige was introduced to drugs at a New York City nightclub when she was sixteen. "It was fun at first," Blige admitted to *Ebony* magazine. According to the annual teen survey Monitoring the Future (MTF), teens say that the main reason to get high is to relax and have a good time. Forty-five percent of teens do not see a great risk in daily drinking. Many teens face huge social pressure to smoke marijuana. Using drugs to have fun, though, can lead to substance abuse. One third of teens admit to drinking alcohol to cope with problems. One in seven teens feels that he or she may have a problem with alcohol.

Though these statistics are alarming, the overall use of alcohol and illicit drug use is going down. This trend may be reversed as more states legalize marijuana, the top drug of choice for today's teens. It still remains illegal to buy or use marijuana for those under the age of twenty-one. Marijuana remains a Schedule I drug under the federal Controlled Substances Act (CSA). What does this label mean?

## Drug Classifications

The CSA puts all substances that are regulated by federal law into one of five categories, called schedules. The placement is based on the drug's medical use and its potential for abuse. Schedule I drugs have a high potential for abuse. They have no accepted medical use in the United States. Examples of Schedule I substances include heroin, lysergic acid diethylamide (LSD), marijuana, and methaqualone.

Some Schedule I drugs are dangerous. Heroin is highly addictive. It has a strong potential for overdose and death. Because users often shoot up with needles, heroin use spreads HIV and hepatitis. LSD is a hallucinogen. It distorts the perception of time and space, producing visions and a feeling of euphoria. Abusers may lose their grasp on reality. The delusions can last many hours.

Heroin use has recently spiked in some parts of the United States. Many heroin users first began abusing prescription pain medications before moving on to harder drugs.

## ADDICTION AND INFECTIOUS DISEASES

Anyone who uses drugs or alcohol is at risk for becoming infected with diseases such as hepatitis and HIV/AIDS. Substance use often lowers inhibitions. Drunk or high teens may engage in behaviors such as unsafe sex that they would not do if sober. Drug abuse also takes a toll on the immune system of the body. Poor nutrition, poor sleep habits, and the impact of toxic substances on vital organs all contribute to a lowered immunity. Those who use and share needles or syringes are at the most risk. The National Institute on Drug Abuse estimates that each injection drug user who has the hepatitis C virus infects twenty other people. Studies by the Centers for Disease Control and Prevention found that the younger the injection drug user, the more he or she shared needles. About one in ten people who inject drugs is infected with HIV/AIDS. Only about 50 percent are aware that they have the disease.

Classifying marijuana as a Schedule I drug is controversial. Some argue that medical marijuana helps those who have appetite loss and nausea as a result of cancer. Marijuana opponents cite research showing the drug's negative effects on adolescent brains. They say that pot is a gateway drug to other illegal drugs. According to NIDA, marijuana dependence has become the number one reason for teens' admissions to rehab.

Schedule II substances also have a high risk of abuse. These drugs, however, have an accepted medical use in the United States. They can lead to severe psychological or physical dependence. Some examples of Schedule II drugs include morphine, phencyclidine (PCP), cocaine (coke), methadone, and methamphetamine (meth). The percentage of teens who use these drugs is small and declining.

Schedule III drugs have a lower potential for abuse than those in Schedules I and II. Drugs in this category include anabolic steroids, codeine, hydrocodone, ketamine, and barbiturates. Some of these drugs, such as OxyContin and Vicodin, are narcotics. They are often prescribed for pain. Teens find them in their parents' medicine cabinets or for sale on the street. They may be prescribed these drugs after a sports injury or surgery. Schedule III barbiturates are used in hospitals as sedatives and anesthetics.

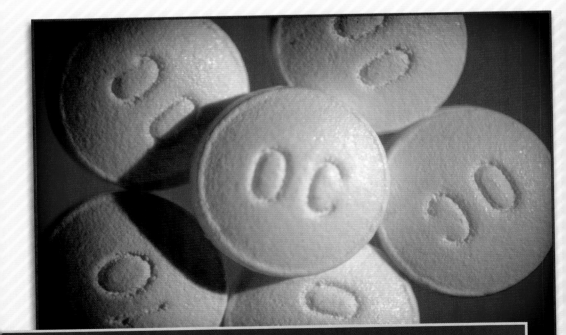

Schedule III prescription pain medications are among the most abused substances by teen users. Opioids such as Vicodin and OcyContin are often prescribed after a sports injury or surgery.

The drugs in Schedule IV are widely prescribed and used. They have a low potential for abuse compared to the lower schedules. Examples of these drugs include Darvon, Equanil, Valium, and Xanax. Doctors prescribe these for anxiety, panic attacks, and sleep disorders. Abusers might take them in combination with other drugs. Or they might take the drugs to counteract the effects of drugs such as meth or coke. The club drug Rohynol (roofies) is in this schedule. Schedule V medications mostly consist of cough medicines with low levels of narcotics in them. The risk of abuse is low.

In addition to being categorized according to their potential for abuse, drugs can be grouped according to their effect on the body. Stimulants speed up the body and brain. Some examples

One of the most dangerous methods of getting high is by inhaling household products such as model glue, acetone, and gasoline. Huffing these substances can cause heart, lung, and brain damage.

include ecstasy, amphetamines, caffeine, nicotine, and cocaine. Depressants slow down the body's normal activity. These drugs include marijuana, opioids, alcohol, barbiturates, and tranquilizers. Hallucinogens such as LSD, PCP, and sometimes ecstasy are mood-altering drugs that affect the brain. Inhalants such as glue, gasoline, and lighter fluid can produce a high. Inhaled substances are often the first illicit drugs that young teens try because they are often found around the house. Though the potential for addiction is low, these drugs are dangerous.

## Stages of Addiction

Teen addicts don't set out to become dependent on drugs. Adolescence is a time of testing limits and trying new experiences. Teens crave excitement and novelty, most often with peers. They experiment with drinking alcohol or smoking pot. Some decide that feeling high is fun and safe. The MTF survey shows that the percentage of students seeing great risk from smoking pot has fallen to its lowest levels since the 1970s. The percent of teens seeing great risk from drinking five or more drinks in a row has risen slightly. The earlier teens begin experimenting with drugs, the greater the risk of addiction.

If taking drugs or drinking alcohol has mostly positive effects, then use will continue. Drinking alcohol, smoking pot, or taking pain pills from a parent's supply may help a teen relax, relieve pain or anxiety, get to sleep, or stay awake.

For most teens, parents discover the use and intervene. Or teens learn on their own that substance use interferes with school or athletic goals, and they stop using. They may even experience a traumatic event, such as becoming sick after binge drinking, being caught driving impaired, or having unsafe sex.

Mary J. Blige turned her life around after a frightening incident when she was twenty-six. She went on to win numerous awards for her records.

Only a small percent of teens move from the occasional and regular use to the risky and dysfunctional use. They become obsessed with getting and using the substance. Their use interferes with family, friends, and school. They often abandon interests and hobbies. They neglect hygiene, nutrition, and basic daily tasks. They become physically dependent on the substance. They find it difficult to function without it. Instead of drinking on the weekends with friends, they begin their day with alcohol and drink all day and evening. Dependent teens are aware of the negative consequences of their use but continue anyway.

Teens who are dependent on drugs or alcohol often isolate themselves from family and friends. Without intervention, they can move into addiction. Family and friends can help stop the behavior before it gets out of control.

Nineteen-year-old Amy tells her story on the National Council on Alcoholism and Drug Dependence (NCADD) website. "My binge drinking began in high school, and with it, blackouts and promiscuous sex," she writes. She brought hard liquor to school in Gatorade bottles. After graduation, her drinking increased.

Alison started drinking at fourteen. She writes, "Alcohol was my drug of choice but I smoked pot, popped pills, used acid, crack, cocaine—whatever I could get my hands on." Twenty-year-old Raja wrote that his hitting bottom "started with drinks before a night out, and it ended in a very small bathroom with a needle in my arm."

The last stage of drug use is addiction. Those with substance use disorder crave their substance. They suffer withdrawal symptoms if they don't have it daily. They have developed a tolerance for the drug. They need more and more just to keep feeling the same high. They often resort to crime, such as selling the drug, to afford their use. Their abuse has become chronic, or long standing. Most teens who become addicted are unable to quit using on their own. They will need the support of friends and family, plus a whole team of medical professionals, to shake their addiction.

# CHAPTER 3

# GETTING CLEAN

One of the hardest experiences anyone can go through is to watch loved ones self-destruct into addiction. At first they may deny that they are alcohol or drug abusers. They will claim that they can quit at any time. As the substance use disorder hijacks the addicts' brain, they become strangers to family and friends. Nothing becomes as important as keeping access to their drugs.

Teens who have an addiction act in destructive ways. Their health deteriorates. They lie and steal to support their habit. They push away family and friends. The addiction causes them to spiral out of control, sometimes even to their death. The list of talented musicians and actors for whom drugs played a large role in ending their life is long: Amy Winehouse, Whitney Houston, Heath Ledger, Philip Seymour Hoffman, Cory Monteith, Dee Dee Ramone, Kurt Cobain, Jimi Hendrix, Jim Morrison, Janis Joplin, Elvis Presley, and many more.

Many teens are sentenced to rehab by drug courts. Drug courts are collaborations among local juvenile justice systems and local substance abuse agencies. Their programs are alternatives to being locked up in juvenile justice facilities. Teens with serious addictions can be ordered to residential programs. Most teens live at home and attend outpatient treatment programs.

## Choosing a Treatment Program

According to NIDA, teens are less likely than adults to feel they need treatment for an addiction. Though a low percentage of teens who need treatment actually get help, the need is vital. The damage being done to maturing brains can be lifelong.

Young substance abusers will try to hide their use from their families. Parents will eventually have to confront the issue. The first step is for families to educate themselves about addiction and treatment. Hotlines, websites, school counselors, and networks of friends and acquaintances can provide information. The U.S. government provides phone numbers and websites dedicated to helping families understand their options. SAMHSA provides a national helpline for treatment referrals at 1-800-662-HELP (4357). The National Alcoholism and Substance Abuse Information Center keeps a database of drug and alcohol treatment centers. Its twenty-four-hour-a-day number is 1-800-784-6776.

The next step is an assessment of the extent of the substance abuse. This screening should be done by a licensed addiction counselor who is also trained in adolescent development. During the assessment, counselors should ask teens about their insight into their substance abuse problems. They should ask about the teens' readiness and motivation to deal with their substance abuse. Counselors should find out about their support system and outside resources, such as sober friends. They

Teens who seek treatment for their substance abuse learn how to manage stress, control their emotions, and set goals. Seeing a school counselor is a great first step.

should assess whether the teens need to undergo detox to get the drugs out of their body. Finally, they should determine if teens have a co-existing mental health issue.

## Dual Diagnosis

Singer Demi Lovato admitted publicly in 2013 that she battled an eating disorder as well as substance abuse. This "dual diagnosis" is common. The National Alliance on Mental Illness reports that half of adolescents with a substance abuse problem also have a mental illness. Some of these include depression, schizophrenia, bipolar disorder, obsessive-compulsive disorder, panic disorder, post-traumatic stress disorder, eating disorders, and high anxiety.

Experts believe that substance abuse and mental illnesses are linked. Teens may try to self-medicate for their mood or anxiety disorder using drugs or alcohol, or they may use drugs to counteract the side effects of the medications they take to treat their mental illness. In some cases, an addict or alcoholic whose problem is out of control may develop depression. Substance abuse changes the chemicals in the brain, throwing them out of balance.

# Types of Treatment

With the results of the assessment, families can decide the best treatment option. They also need to consider their financial and medical insurance situation. Since 2008, mental health treatment for chronic illness must be covered at the same level as physical health. Parents and guardians should research a variety of treatment settings, types of treatment, and services available both during and after treatment. Options include residential programs, outpatient programs, and individual therapy.

## Residential Treatment

Treatment in a residential facility helps teens who have the most serious addictions, such as those from opioids or cocaine. They may lack resources at home or need a medically supervised detox. Most adult rehabs have separate programs and living quarters for teens. There are residential rehab facilities specifically for teens. Clients typically stay for thirty to sixty days. Contact with family is limited.

After becoming physically stabilized, clients participate in individual and group therapy. Most use a twelve-step approach, such as the Alcoholics Anonymous (AA) model. Educational programs are provided for those still in high school. Most provide recreation, such as horseback riding, sports, and crafts. Still, Anne Fletcher, author of *Inside Rehab*, finds that a big problem at residential rehabs is boredom.

One advantage of residential rehab is that clients are away from the triggers and stressors that led to the substance abuse. Treatment focuses on behavior, emotions, and life skills. There may be separate wings or sessions for young men and women. Those with less serious addictions are sometimes kept in different groups from those with more serious or long-standing abuse. Family therapy is integrated into the program, though that may be limited by distance. These facilities can cost up to $1,000 per day.

Residential treatment is expensive and lasts for many weeks. It is important to choose a place that is a good match for a particular young patient. Here are some questions to ask before choosing a residential treatment facility:

1. How will my child's substance problem be assessed?
2. What types of therapies are offered?
3. What qualifications do your staff have?
4. How do your programs deal with dual diagnosis?
5. How is the family involved in treatment?
6. What are the rules and the consequences for breaking them?
7. How will you follow up with my child after treatment?
8. How do you know that your programs are effective?

# ALTERNATIVE THERAPIES

Yoga can be a good complement to other, more traditional forms of therapy.

Grooming a gentle horse. Meditating in a garden. Acting in a drama. Shaping a pot on a wheel. Drumming in a circle. Alternative therapies such as these are finding their way into substance abuse treatment programs. Mindfulness meditation decreases cravings and improves sleep. Playing music decreases depression, stress, anxiety and anger. Feeding, grooming, and exercising horses improves emotional control and feelings of self-worth. Other alternative therapies include the creative arts, sports and exercise, yoga, and nutritional treatments. While none of these activities can take the place of traditional treatment, numerous small studies show benefits. All of these therapies should only be used under the supervision of experts in these fields.

## Outpatient Treatment

Not every teen with an addiction needs hospitalization and residential treatment. Over 80 percent of teens are treated as outpatients. For many substance abusers, outpatient treatment has several advantages. The programs are likely to be less expensive and won't drain family financial resources. It is easier to involve families, who are crucial to treatment success. Teens can stay connected to the positive elements in their community, integrate into local self-help groups they can attend after their intensive treatment ends, and better coordinate with school and probation officers.

Whether teens attend residential or outpatient treatment facilities, they all should have access to programs that have evidence that they are successful. Fletcher finds that family therapy, cognitive-behavioral therapy (CBT), and motivational interviewing are the most effective approaches.

One family member's substance abuse can throw the whole family into turmoil. Family therapy can help all family members recover and heal. This therapy can take place on an outpatient basis.

Family therapy uses the emotional ties among family members to support the teen. CBT focuses on the relationships among a person's thoughts, feelings, and behaviors. A counselor might ask a client to explore the thinking that leads to self-destructive actions. During a motivational interviewing conversation, a counselor tries to strengthen a young person's own motivation and commitment to change.

Most rehab programs use a combination of group and individual counseling. Clients may participate in up to nine hours of group counseling each week. Group sessions are cost effective for rehab programs. Counselors give their clients assignments, often based on reading about a topic.  Topics might include

Group counseling allows teens to talk to other teens and adults about the issues that led to their substance abuse. They learn how to express their emotions in a safe environment.

coping with triggers and cravings and avoiding relapse. In a group session, participants discuss their ideas. During weekly one-on-one sessions with therapists, teens can talk about their personal problems. They might explore the reasons why their drug use escalated into abuse. They can work to resolve long-standing issues.

Effective rehab programs help teens to develop and improve coping and problem-solving skills. They provide teens with opportunities to learn to control their emotions and adapt to different social situations. Teens learn stress management. They learn to set goals for themselves that lead to independence and sobriety. Alison writes, "I learned better coping skills, enabling me to deal with issues and problems as they came up without using drugs." Looking back at her rehab, Amy writes, "In recovery I have witnessed a miracle in myself. I have been given a new life." Raja agrees. He writes, "I am the man I want to be today."

# CHAPTER 4

# STAYING CLEAN

Teens with drug or alcohol dependence face huge obstacles during treatment. They work to overcome cravings. They confront their past failures. They learn about the science of addiction. They prepare to re-enter school and community. During treatment they learn that substance abuse is a chronic illness. They may never recover from their disease. They will need an aftercare program to maintain their recovery. But only about 10 percent of teens start a continuing care program after treatment. At least 50 percent of teens relapse back into substance use during the first ninety days after completing rehab.

Effective aftercare programs provide a variety of elements to keep teens clean and sober. Regular individual and family counseling, group therapy, drug testing, recreation with sober friends, and twelve-step or alternative programs can keep teens focused on recovery. Most teens will need to go back to school. They may have to let parents monitor their friends, Internet and phone use, homework, and spending money. For teens who are old enough, a job might be useful.

# Individual and Family Therapy

An insightful therapist is an important part of an aftercare team. The therapist should be certified in both adolescent therapy and drug and alcohol counseling. Counselors need to pass certifying exams in the state in which they practice. Parents and teens can tap into their networks of family and friends for referrals. They can get referrals from their inpatient or outpatient rehab facility. Local hospitals, universities, and state and county mental health clinics often provide counseling on a sliding scale.

A trained therapist can help teens find resources for recovery and beyond. Teens can set goals to finish high school and look for employment or higher education.

Training, experience, and degrees are important in choosing a drug and alcohol counselor. Even more important is the trust and connection that teens establish with their counselor. An empathetic therapist can break through the defenses that many teens have built up throughout their lives. In the beginning of aftercare, the therapist will want to meet weekly. After several months, the time between meetings may be extended to biweekly or monthly.

The therapist may want teen clients to continue with group therapy. An accepting group may be a place of growth and healing. Teens can learn to relate to each other sober and practice valuable communication skills. Weekly group meetings may continue as long as teens need their support.

Some counselors confront their young clients. They purposely challenge them to face their failures. They may do this in front of peers. This approach can backfire. Fletcher says that "strategies designed to make teens feel bad, embarrassed, or ashamed are not beneficial, may be harmful, and don't help them to change." The therapist-client relationship should be based on respect.

An important part of aftercare for teens is family therapy. Family relationships can be damaged by addiction. A skilled therapist can help teens, their parents, and their siblings reconnect. Families can share honest feelings about their issues. Teens can try to explain why they began using and what it took

DRY DRUNK

Those who spend time in the world of alcohol rehab know the term "dry drunk." It is an insult used against people who do not seem to have learned anything during rehab. Though they are sober, they refuse to work on issues of anger, denial, and blame. Instead of using new challenges to grow, they wallow in self-pity and remember their drinking days. Actor Drew Barrymore recalled in *People* magazine that when she came out of rehab at age thirteen, "I didn't want to face that I was still as much an addict as when I first went to the hospital. Even though I had not been drinking or doing drugs, I had still been hanging around with a crowd that did." Family and friends can help dry drunks by encouraging them to attend self-help groups. There they can find positive strategies to cope with problems.

for them to stop. Both parents and teens can practice active listening and conflict resolution. The therapist can help parents set rules regarding school, use of cellphone and social media, and socializing. Parents may also want time alone with a therapist to deal with the stresses they may be facing.

## Twelve-Step Programs

Teens in both residential and outpatient alcohol abuse programs most likely will have been introduced to a twelve-step program. The first such program was Alcoholics Anonymous (AA). Most large communities also have twelve-step programs for a variety of substances, such as Narcotics Anonymous (NA). The steps encourage people who want to stop drinking to admit powerlessness over alcohol. They ask God to help them admit their failures and make amends to those they have hurt.

Teens may be encouraged to use twelve-step programs to maintain their sobriety. For many teens, these programs work well. Fletcher's review of research shows that teens who get involved in AA and NA after treatment "are much more likely to remain abstinent than those who don't." Twelve-step meetings offer newly sober people a safe place where others understand their problems. Meetings, offered at all times of the day in most cities, prevent isolation and provide fellowship. No one is judged. Members interpret "God" in personal ways. For some, the higher power is spiritual, not religious. They may think of the higher power as nature, one's life force, or the power of the group itself.

Some teens and their parents have concerns about twelve-step programs. Most meetings are attended by adults, some of whom have disturbing pasts. Teens may develop relationships with strangers without adult supervision. Fletcher quotes an AA

AA meetings are free, and most are open to anyone. At a typical meeting, participants discuss a topic chosen by a group leader. But AA is not for everyone. There are several recovery programs that are successful alternatives to AA.

attendee who says that "just because people are sober doesn't mean they are good people."

Teens may not have a strong belief in God and balk at the emphasis on religious belief. They may not want to think of themselves as powerless to make change by themselves. Most cities have alternatives to AA. Organizations such as Secular Organizations for Sobriety (SOS), SMART Recovery, and Women for Sobriety put more emphasis on personal responsibility.

## Drug Testing

Asking teens to undergo random drug testing may be part of the contract parents and teens draw up after addiction treatment.

At-home testing kits might seem convenient. However, most experts recommend a urinalysis at a medical facility. At a lab, teens will be carefully supervised. A professional test is less likely to produce false positives or negatives.

Teens might accuse their parents of not trusting them if drug tests are required. However, teens can use the threat of testing as an out when they are pressured to use by their peers. A dirty test is evidence that a teen is relapsing. With this warning, families and therapists can step in and intervene before the substance abuse gets worse.

## Socializing After Recovery

After treatment, most teens will want to resume their normal life. They will want to hang out with friends to relax and have fun. Going back to the same social situations in which they abused drugs or alcohol is dangerous. Old friends and hangouts could easily trigger a relapse. The website KidsHealth.org has tips to help teens maintain their hard-won sobriety, summarized below:

- Find friends who support your decision to stay sober.
- Identify family and friends who can be available when you need them. They want to help you get through the tough times.
- Plan activities that take place in settings that are drug- and alcohol-free. Go to a movie, a school activity, or a friend's house to play video games. Avoid parties where alcohol may be served.
- Have a plan if you do end up in a place where alcohol or drugs are used. Your counselor or a family member can role-play different scenarios that can happen. Practicing refusal skills ahead of time can help head off temptations.
- If you do backslide into old behaviors, don't be ashamed. Talk to a trusted adult who can help you get back on track.

# Going Back to School

Teens who took time off school to attend treatment will eventually have to return. They may be worried about how they will fit back in. Will their friends judge them and label them as addicts? Will they be able to make up classes and graduate on time? Will they be able to avoid the minefield of triggers and cravings?

Some teens might want to consider going to a new school. Though it may be stressful to make new friends and meet new teachers, a new school will allow a fresh start. Some communities have alternative schools and recovery high schools. These schools have more supports in place for teens who are dealing with difficult issues. They may also have options, such as online courses, to make up classes and credits lost during treatment. Attending an online high school may be an option, especially for teens who are far behind or fear the stigma of being labeled a drug addict or alcoholic. Teens will need a lot of self-discipline to work at home alone on a computer.

A recovery high school helped fifteen-year-old Lucy Gross stay sober after spending seven months in a residential rehab, according to a 2009 CNN report. "Recovery high, the real gift that it gives to the kids is the soft landing when they come out of rehab," says Lucy's father, Tony Gross. Students attend group sessions and take weekly random drug tests. Lucy's school has a 90 percent graduation rate.

Whatever school teens decide to attend, they need to work with the school's mental health team. Counselors can identify adult mentors at school who would be willing to provide support. Getting involved in sports, clubs, and activities will help teens make new friends and stay busy. Volunteer work increases self-esteem and releases endorphins in the brain that some call a

Returning to school after undergoing treatment can be a difficult transition. One solution is recovery high school. Alternative high schools for students in recovery incorporate group sessions in the curriculum. Students support each other in their efforts to stay sober.

"helper's high." Teens who set achievable goals for life after high school can find motivation to stay sober and focus on academics.

## Technology Help During Recovery

Teens today seem glued to their phones. They check in with parents, update social media accounts, find friends' where-abouts, and even get homework assignments. It is no surprise that their phone can be a friend in sobriety. Cellphone apps can help teens manage triggers and emotions. Some apps provide encouragement, relaxation, and goal setting. Other apps teach visualization and relaxation techniques. Teens can set reminders about attending appointments and group meetings. Most of the apps are free or low cost and are available on multiple platforms. For those who find support in twelve-step programs, there are several apps to download. The 12 Steps AA Companion holds a searchable Big Book, a variety of prayers, a place to jot and share notes, links to AA offices, and buttons to contact fellow members and sponsors. The AA Big Book and More offers daily encouraging messages. AA Speakers to Go allows members to listen to talks from inspiring speakers. Friend of Jimmy provides recovery messages for members of NA. Recoverize.com, for both AA and NA members, includes daily readings, speakers to listen to, a chat room, and inspirational recovery stories. Some popular apps can find and provide times and maps to meetings.

There are plenty of apps not associated with twelve-step programs that provide inspiration and motivation. For example, the Mindfulness App provides guided meditation sessions, helpful to distract from cravings. Breathe2Relax can help with stress and sleep. Twenty-Four Hours a Day was developed by the Hazelden Treatment programs. Its collection of prayers and meditations can help newly sober teens make good decisions during challenging times. Afternoon Affirmations sends a calming message every day at 1:00 p.m.

One app that was tested but is not yet available for wide use is called A-CHESS. Its GPS issues an alert if smartphone owners get near a place that could set off a trigger. A "panic button" gives instant access to reminders, distractions, or supportive friends. It also provides access to online support groups and counselors.

A web-based program called Therapeutic Education System (TES) includes interactive video simulations. It has "what if" scenarios to teach refusal skills. One video shows the importance of a young woman's body language in convincing friends she does not want the drugs her friends are offering.

Some young adults put together music playlists that help them through tough moments. Rapper Eminem's 2010 album *Recovery* contains songs such as "Going Through Changes." He sings, "When inside, I'm dying, I am finally realizing I need help/I can't do it by myself." Pink wonders, "But how do I feel this good sober?" in her song "Sober." Fans can find motivating music by Macklemore and Ryan Lewis, Staind, the Red Hot Chili Peppers, and the Eagles to listen to. Drugs are often part of the music scene. Many musicians choose sobriety before they hit bottom.

Teens who like spending time on the Internet will find a wealth of resources to support sobriety. Most recovery organizations have a Facebook presence and a website. Twelve-step programs host online meetings, forums, and chat rooms. Blogs written by people who honestly describe their struggles and achievements can encourage former substance abusers. There is a whole community of people of all ages available to cheer the efforts of those in recovery.

# CHAPTER 5

# MY FAMILY NEEDS HELP

"**M**y biggest regret about growing up with my dad is that I lost so many opportunities. Most of all, I lost the opportunity to feel like I was a lovable human being. I lost the opportunity to do well in school, because I was constantly fighting sadness or anger or depression."

This was written by a teen named Greg. He documented his life in the 2013 book *When Addiction Hits Home*. Greg, like millions of other children and teens in the United States, has a family member with a substance abuse problem. Substance abuse crosses through ethnicity, cultural backgrounds, income levels, and educational levels. A family member who abuses drugs or alcohol can have devastating effects on the rest of the family.

## Substance-Abusing Parents

When parents abuse drugs or alcohol, family life can become chaotic and unpredictable. Family rules and structure may be

Substance-abusing parents can create a family life that is chaotic and confusing. Children may not understand the source of the problem and may blame themselves for their parents' behaviors.

inconsistent. Children don't understand that their parents' moods and behaviors are determined by the amount of drugs or alcohol they have in their bodies. This situation can make children feel confused. They have conflicting feelings of love, worry, and anger at the abusing parent. These feelings become more intense if no one talks about the substance abuse. After a while, children may try to block their emotions and not feel anything.

Some children blame themselves for their parent's addiction. An out-of-control mom or dad may accuse the children

Children of alcoholics or drug addicts are sometimes forced to take on the adult roles of running the household. They may take responsibility for younger siblings and end up taking care of the parents.

of being too loud, messy, dumb, or careless, and that is what causes the drinking. Children may try to compensate by getting straight As or keeping the house perfectly clean. They often become overachievers. They also may withdraw from friends and try to hide their family's problems. Other parents may warn against befriending the children of alcoholics or drug abusers.

The parent's substance abuse may lead to a variety of health problems, unemployment, criminal behavior, divorce, and domestic abuse. Dysfunctional parenting can lead to children taking on adult roles. Teens may try to take care of younger children. They take on the responsibility of feeding, clothing, and supervising them. They also end up taking care of the parent. Psychologists call this "parentification." The constant stress can lead to depression, anxiety, and low self-esteem.

In a 2014 article, journalist Alana Levinson wrote about "the 'invisible losses' suffered by children of addicts: loss of love, stability, a caretaker, a carefree childhood." Because substance abuse is often thought to be a problem of choice and morals, there is little community support.

Robert Munsch is the author of *The Paper Bag Princess* and other popular children's books. He is also a recovering alcoholic. Here is his message in the introduction to *When Addiction Hits Home:*

> If your mom, or dad, or sibling, or aunt, or grandpa is an addict, you didn't cause their addiction and you can't cure it. If they make appointments with you and don't keep them, that's not your fault. If you talk to them and they don't listen, that's not your fault. If you have a family member who's an addict, that's not your fault. Staying away from drugs and alcohol and realizing that you can't "fix" or "cure" an addict may be the only way to ensure that you live your own life, and not theirs. But that doesn't mean you can't still love them.

LGBT ISSUES

Teens who identify as gay, lesbian, bisexual, or transgender use and abuse drugs and alcohol at a greater rate than straight teens, SAMHSA reports. One reason is that LGBT youth may use drugs and alcohol to cope with the discrimination and homophobia they find in their communities. They often face rejection by family and peers. They struggle with self-esteem and identity issues. They may self-medicate to treat depression. LGBT youth also seek treatment at a lower rate than straight teens. There are few inpatient or outpatient programs that specifically meet the needs of the LGBT community. Gay community centers and websites that focus on the health care needs of LGBT adolescents and adults are good places to look for treatment referrals.

# Sibling Substance Abuse

Sibling substance abuse has a harmful impact on children and teens. Parents may be in denial about one of their children's addiction. The substance abuse can escalate until a crisis forces the parents to confront the issue. The abusing child may experience an arrest or an overdose. When this happens, family resources shift to the crisis. Parents spend time and money on medical care or legal help. Their energy and attention is devoted to the substance-abusing sibling. The other children learn to take care of themselves, while keeping secrets from friends. Their own needs are neglected. They may feel anger, jealousy, and guilt.

The whole family is affected when one family member abuses drugs or alcohol. Siblings often feel neglected when family resources are directed to the substance abuser. Parents may spend more time and energy on the sibling in trouble.

*When Addiction Hits Home* writer Nicola also experienced a family member's substance abuse. Her brother Kevin started drinking in elementary school. She describes the disruption he caused in their home. "When he couldn't manipulate people to get his way, he would become furious with them. The personality switch was as immediate as turning on a lightbulb. He had my mom and me walking on eggshells all the time."

There are several different organizations that can provide support for teens living with substance abuse that is not their own. The websites of recovery programs such as AA, NA, and SMART Recovery provide links to resources for family and friends of substance abusers. Most of these organizations sponsor meetings for family members in larger communities.

Family members can find support in groups such as Al-Anon. In group meetings, participants share stories about their own experiences with a substance-abusing parent, child, sibling, or friend.

Most offer chat rooms and message boards for those who want or need to connect online. Alateen hosts meetings where teens can meet peers who have alcoholic family members. There they can talk freely about what has been kept hidden. Other teens validate their feelings. They can also chat through the Alateen website.

## SUPPORTING A FRIEND WHO IS ABUSING DRUGS

It is not easy to confront a friend about his or her drug use. Many people with substance abuse problems don't want to admit they have a problem. So what can you do?

• **Stay safe:** Don't ride in a car when a drunk friend is driving. Don't confront a friend when he or she is abusing, especially if there is a chance of violence.

• **Use a supportive, caring tone, even if you are angry.**

• **Don't call your friend out in front of others.** It is not your job to make someone else's business public.

• **Plan what to say.** Hotlines and websites can give you specific information so you can lay out the facts. Let your friend know that while you still care, the risks he or she is taking scare you.

• **Be a good listener.** Your friend may open up if he or she feels heard.

• **While you can be a good friend, know what you can't do.** You can't solve your friends' problems. You can't make them stop abusing drugs or alcohol. You can't make them ask for treatment.

The impact of living in a family with substance abuse can be lifelong. Children of alcoholics and drug abusers are more at risk of becoming substance abusers as well. As adults they have increased rates of divorce and violence. They have a greater tendency to suffer from mental disorders such as depression and anxiety.

Although children with parents or siblings who abuse substances are at risk for negative outcomes, there are positive effects. Children develop resiliency. They bounce back from failure. They practice coping skills that allow them to deal with both major and minor obstacles in life. They develop tools to manage stress and disruption. They learn to take on responsibility and make decisions. With counseling, family members of substance abusers can grow in a healthy way.

Defeating drug and alcohol addiction can seem overwhelming. Most substance abusers cycle through periods of abuse and recovery before they achieve lasting recovery. With treatment, teens who are caught in these cycles can become successful adults. They need communities to step up and provide effective programs. They need treatment that focuses on education and growth. They need technology that provides inspiration as well as distraction. They need caring counselors. They need their families' support. Will all of these elements in place, young addicts and alcoholics can find sobriety.

# Glossary

**AFFIRMATION** A positive statement about oneself.

**BIPOLAR DISORDER** A mental disorder in which a person alternates between depression and mania.

**CHROMOSOME** The part of a cell that contains the genes, which control how the organism grows.

**COLLABORATION** Working with other people to achieve a goal.

**COMPULSIVITY** Not able to stop or control doing something.

**DYSFUNCTIONAL** Unable to act or function normally.

**ENDORPHINS** Substances in the brain that act like pain killers or mood enhancers.

**EUPHORIA** A feeling of great happiness and excitement.

**HALLUCINOGEN** A drug that causes people to sense things that are not real.

**HIPPOCAMPUS** The part of the brain that forms, stores, and processes memory.

**HOMOPHOBIA** A fear, dislike, or discrimination against homosexuals.

**ILLICIT** Unlawful or illegal.

**INFECTIOUS** Capable of being spread from one person to another.

**INHIBITION** Unconscious restraint of behavior due to guilt or fear.

**NEUROTRANSMITTER** A chemical substance in the brain that transmits nerve impulses.

**OBSESSIVE-COMPULSIVE DISORDER** A personality disorder characterized by constant unwanted thoughts and behaviors.

**PREDISPOSITION** A tendency to a condition or quality, based on genetic and environmental factors.

**RELAPSE** To fall back into a former state or behavior; to backslide.

**RESILIENCY** The ability to recover easily from illness, depression, or adversity.

**SCHIZOPHRENIA** A severe mental illness characterized by delusions, hallucinations, and disorganized speech and behavior.

## For More Information

Alcoholics Anonymous (AA)
P.O. Box 459
New York, NY 10163
(212) 870-3400
Website: http://www.aa.org
AA is a worldwide fellowship of sober alcoholics. The organi-
    zation uses a twelve-step method to encourage recovery.

Canadian Centre on Substance Abuse (CCSA)
75 Albert Street, Suite 500
Ottawa, ON K1P 5E7
Canada
(613) 235-4048
Website: http://www.ccsa.ca
CCSA works to minimize the harm associated with the use of
    alcohol, tobacco, and other drugs by disseminating infor-
    mation about drug abuse. It supports organizations
    involved in substance abuse treatment, prevention, and
    education.

Narcotics Anonymous (NA)
P.O. Box 9999
Van Nuys, CA 91409
(818) 773-9999
Website: http://www.na.org
This organization supports recovering drug addicts who
    meet regularly to help each other abstain from drugs.

National Alliance on Mental Illness (NAMI)
3803 N. Fairfax Drive, Suite 100
Arlington, VA 22203
(703) 524-7600
Website: http://www.nami.org/
NAMI provides resources for sufferers of dual diagnosis, both
   a mental illness and a substance abuse problem.

National Council on Alcoholism and Drug Dependence
   (NCADD)
244 East 58th Street, 4th Floor
New York, NY 10022
(212) 269-7797
Website: http://www.ncadd.org
NCADD is a volunteer health organization that helps indi-
   viduals overcome addictions. It also develops substance
   abuse prevention and education programs for youth.

National Institute on Alcohol Abuse and Alcoholism (NIAAA)
5635 Fishers Lane, MSC 9304
Bethesda, MD 20892-9304
(301) 443-3869
Website: http://www.niaaa.nih.gov
NIAAA conducts research into alcoholism and disseminates
   its findings to the public.

National Institute on Drug Abuse (NIDA)
6001 Executive Boulevard, Room 5213
Bethesda, MD 20892-9561
(301) 443-1124
Website: http://www.drugabuse.gov

NIDA conducts research on drug abuse in order to improve
addiction prevention, treatment, and policy efforts.

National Institute of Mental Health (NIMH)
Science Writing, Press, and Dissemination Branch
6001 Executive Boulevard, Room 6200, MSC 9663
Bethesda, MD 20892-9663
(866) 615-6464
Website: http://www.nimh.nih.gov/index.shtml
NIMH provides resources and information about how mental
illnesses can be treated and prevented.

Rational Recovery
P.O. Box 800
Lotus, CA 95651
(530) 621-2667
Website: https://rational.org
Rational Recovery is a national self-help organization that
offers a cognitive rather than spiritual approach to recovery from alcoholism. Its philosophy holds that alcoholics
can attain sobriety without depending on other people
or a "higher power."

SMART Recover Canada
223 12 Avenue SW
Calgary, AB T2R 0G9
Canada
(403) 619-4210
Website: http://www.smartrecovery.ca
SMART Recovery Canada provides free self-help programs
dedicated to addiction recovery.

Substance Abuse and Mental Health Services Administration
(SAMHSA)
1 Choke Cherry Road
Rockville, MD 20857
(877) 726-4727
Website: http://www.samhsa.gov
SAMHSA provides information, research, and services to
those working to reduce the impact of substance abuse
and mental illness on America's communities.

## Websites

Because of the changing nature of Internet links, Rosen
Publishing has developed an online list of websites related to
the subject of this book. This site is updated regularly. Please
use this link to access this list:

http://www.rosenlinks.com/ESS/Addict

# For Further Reading

Carlson, Hannah. *Addiction: The Brain Disease*. Branford, CT: Bick Publishing, 2010.

Espojo, Roman, ed. *Chemical Dependence* (Opposing Viewpoints Series). Farmington Hills, MI: Greenhaven Press, 2011.

Foote, Jeffrey, Carrie Wilkens, and Nicole Kosanke. *Beyond Addiction: How Science and Kindness Help People Change*. New York, NY: Scribner, 2014.

Hari, Johann. *Chasing the Scream: The First and Last Days of the War on Drugs.* New York, NY: Bloomsbury, 2015.

Haugen, David, and Susan Musser, ed. *Addiction* (Introducing Issues with Opposing Viewpoints). Farmington Hills, MI: Greenhaven Press, 2013.

Higgins, Melissa. *Living with Substance Addiction* (Living with Health Challenges). Edina, MN: Essential Library/ABDO, 2012.

Hopkins, Ellen. *Fallout* (Crank Book 3). New York, NY: Margaret K. McElderry Books, 2010.

Hunnycutt, Susan, ed. *Interventions* (Opposing Viewpoints Series). Farmington Hills, MI: Greenhaven Press, 2012.

Kuhar, Michael. *The Addicted Brain: Why We Abuse Drugs, Alcohol, and Nicotine*. Upper Saddle River, NJ: Pearson Education, 2012.

Miller, Malinda. *Dual Diagnosis: Drug Addiction and Mental Illness*. Broomall, PA: Mason Crest, 2013.

Sanna, E. J. *Heroin and Other Opioids: Poppies' Perilous Children* (Illicit and Misused Drugs). Broomall, PA: Mason Crest Publishers, 2012.

Shantz-Hilkes, Chloe, ed. *Hooked: When Addiction Hits Home.* Toronto, ON: Annick Press, 2013.

Sheff, Nic. *We All Fall Down: Living with Addiction.* New York, NY: Little, Brown and Company, 2012.

Walker, Ida. *Addiction in America: Society, Psychology, and Heredity* (Illicit and Misused Drugs). Broomall, PA: Mason Crest Publishers, 2012.

Wolny, Philip. *The Truth About Heroin* (Drugs & Consequences). New York, NY: Rosen Publishing, 2014.

# Bibliography

Addiction Recovery Guide. "Mobile Apps for Addiction."
March 13, 2015. Retrieved April 28, 2015 (http://www.
addictionrecoveryguide.org/resources/mobile_apps).

American Psychiatric Association. "Substance-Related and
Addictive Disorders." American Psychiatric Publishing,
2013. Retrieved April 27, 2015 (http://www.dsm5.org/
Documents/Substance%20Use%20Disorder%20Fact%20
Sheet.pdf).

Centers for Disease Control and Prevention. "HIV Infection
and HIV-Associated Behaviors Among Injecting Drug
Users—20 Cities, United States, 2009." March 2, 2012.
Retrieved April 11, 2015 (http://www.cdc.gov/mmwr/
preview/mmwrhtml/mm6108a1.htm).

Chappell, Kevin. "Mary J. Blige Talks About Marriage, Her
Triumph Over Drugs, and the Day That Changed Her
Life." *Ebony* magazine, June 2000.

Cunningham, John, Kypros Kypri, and Jim McCambridge. "The
Use of Emerging Technologies in Alcohol Treatment."
*Alcohol Research & Health*, Vol. 33, No. 4, 2011.

Fletcher, Anne. *Inside Rehab*. New York, NY: Viking, 2013.

France, Lisa Respers, and Breeanna Hare. "Zac Efron and
Other Celebs We Didn't Know Battled Addiction." CNN,
September 18, 2013. Retrieved March 29, 2015 (http://
www.cnn.com/2013/09/18/showbiz/celebrity-news-gossip/
zac-efron-rehab-confessions).

Genetic Science Learning Center. "Genes and Addiction."
Retrieved March 29, 2015 (http://learn.genetics.utah.edu/
content/addiction/genes/).

Holland, Kimberly. "The Best Alcoholism iPhone & Android Apps." Healthline, May 21, 2014. Retrieved April 28, 2015 (http://www.healthline.com/health-slideshow/top-alcoholism-iphone-android-apps).

KidsHealth.org. "Dealing with Addiction." 2011. Retrieved April 24, 2015 (http://kidshealth.org/teen/your_mind/friends/addictions.html#).

Levinson, Alana. "Surviving the Secret Childhood Trauma of a Parent's Drug Addiction." *Pacific Standard*, November 20, 2014. Retrieved April 26, 2015 (http://www.psmag.com/health-and-behavior/surviving-secret-childhood-trauma-parents-drug-addiction-94354).

Miller, Malinda. *Dual Diagnosis: Drug Addiction and Mental Illness*. Broomall, PA: Mason Crest, 2013.

Moberg, D. Paul, and Andrew Finch. "Recovery High Schools." *Journal of Groups in Addiction & Recovery*, October 2008.

Monitoring the Future. "2014 Overview Key Findings on Adolescent Drug Use." The University of Michigan Institute for Social Research, 2015. Retrieved April 9, 2015 (http://www.monitoringthefuture.org//pubs/monographs/mtf-overview2014.pdf).

National Alliance on Mental Illness. "Dual Diagnosis: Substance Abuse and Mental Illness." January 2013. Retrieved April 30, 2015 (http://www2.nami.org/Content/NavigationMenu/Inform_Yourself/About_Mental_Illness/By_Illness/Dual_Diagnosis_Substance_Abuse_and_Mental_Illness.htm).

National Institute on Drug Abuse. "Principles of Adolescent Substance Use Disorder Treatment: A Research-Based Guide." January 2014. Retrieved April 12, 2015 (https://www.drugabuse.gov/sites/default/files/podata_1_17_14.pdf).

National Institute on Drug Abuse. "The Science of Drug Abuse and Addiction: The Basics." September 2014. Retrieved April 6, 2015 (http://www.drugabuse.gov/publications/media-guide/science-drug-abuse-addiction-basics).

National Institute on Drug Abuse. "What to Do If You Have a Problem with Drugs: For Teens and Young Adults." June 2014. Retrieved March 29, 2015 (http://www.drugabuse.gov/related-topics/treatment/what-to-do-if-you-have-problem-drugs-teens-young-adults).

Partnership at Drugfree.org. "2010 Partnership Attitude Tracking Study: Teens and Parents." April 6, 2011. Retrieved March 29, 2015 (http://www.drugfree.org/wp-content/uploads/2014/05/FULL-REPORT-FINAL-PATS-Teens-and-Parent-April-6-2011-1.pdf).

Peters, Sarah. "Recovery: There's an App for That." The Fix, February 19, 2014. Retrieved March 29, 2015 (http://www.thefix.com/content/technology-and-addiction).

Shantz-Hilkes, Chloe, ed. Hooked: When Addiction Hits Home. New York, NY: Annick Press, 2013.

Spero, Jesse. "Demi Lovato Reveals: I Would 'Smuggle' Cocaine on Planes." Access Hollywood, December 10, 2013.

Substance Abuse and Mental Health Services Administration. "Results from the 2013 National Survey on Drug Use and Health: Summary of National Findings." Rockville, MD: Substance Abuse and Mental Health Services Administration, 2014. HHS Publication No. (SMA) 14-4887. NSDUH Series H-49.

Swanson, Jeanene. "13 Valuable Alternative Treatments for Addiction." The Fix, September 8, 2014. Retrieved April 28, 2015 (http://www.thefix.com/content/therapies-outside-box?page=all).

Teen Rehab. "Factors to See If Your Child Is at Risk for Addiction." March 10, 2013. Retrieved March 29, 2015 (http://www.teendrugrehabs.com/).

Thompson, Dennis. "Smartphone App May Help People Overcome Alcoholism." HealthDay, March 26, 2014. Retrieved April 27, 2015 (http://consumer.healthday.com/mental-health-information-25/addiction-news-6/alcoholism-app-686184.html).

U.S. Department of Health and Human Services. "Behavioral Health Barometer, United States, 2014." Substance Abuse and Mental Health Services Administration, 2015. Retrieved March 15, 2015 (http://www.samhsa.gov/data/sites/default/files/National_BHBarometer_2014/National_BHBarometer_2014.pdf).

U.S. Department of Justice Drug Enforcement Division. "Controlled Substance Schedules." Retrieved April 10, 2015 (http://www.deadiversion.usdoj.gov/schedules/index.html).

Vimont, Celia. "Technology Shows Promise in Substance Use Prevention and Treatment." Partnership for Drug-Free Kids, October 18, 2011. Retrieved March 29, 2015 (http://www.drugfree.org/join-together/technology-shows-promise-in-substance-use-prevention-and-treatment/).

Young, Saundra. "Recovery High School a 'Soft Landing' for Post-rehab Teens." CNN, April 14, 2009. Retrieved April 27, 2015 (http://www.cnn.com/2009/HEALTH/04/13/addiction.recovery.school.teens/index.html?eref=time_us).

# Index

# About the Author

Susan Henneberg writes about topics of interest to teens and young adults, such as sexual assault, social media, academic success, paranormal experiences, and new technology. She has taught high school and college for over thirty years. A parent of three daughters, she lives in Reno, Nevada.

# Photo Credits